31 LYNSTOCK CRESCENT
NETHY BRIDGE
INVERNESS-SHIRE
PH25 3DX
TEL. (047 982) 325

BANJAXED

TERRY WOGAN

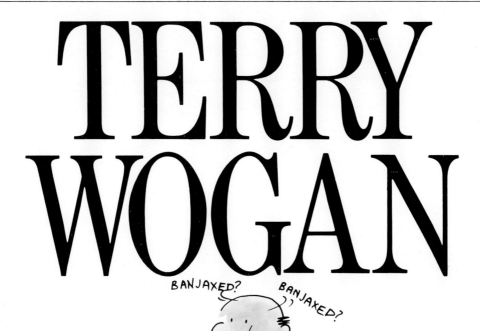

BANJAXED

Varicose utterances by himself,
with selected responses from the listening audience   **Illustrations by Frank Dickens**

Macdonald General Books
Macdonald & Jane's · London & Sydney

First published in 1979 by
Macdonald General Books
Macdonald & Jane's Publishers Ltd
Paulton House
8 Shepherdess Walk
London N1 7LW

Copyright © Terry Wogan 1979

ISBN 0354 08563 8

Made by Lennard Books
31 Bedford Row
London WC1R 4HE

Editor Michael Leitch
Art Director David Pocknell
Designer Michael Cavers
Production Reynolds Clark Associates Limited
Printed and bound in Spain by
Novograph SA, Madrid
Dep Legal M 27646/1979

The author and publishers are grateful to the owners of
copyright material for kindly granting permission for its
use in the book. Every effort has been made to trace the
authors of contributions included, and thanks and
apologies are extended to anyone who for any reason may
not have been contacted.

Contents

Contents

Contents

Preface

When asked how he manages to 'keep so cheerful' in the early mornings, Terry Wogan restrains the natural urge to strike the questioner a blow to the mazzard, and puts his bonny temperament down to clean living, and eating his crusts as a child.

Pressed for a more comprehensive answer, and I wouldn't advise it, the ageing funster will admit to the occasional small cloud blighting his horizon, such as the back of Jimmy Young's head, but our hero's normally sunny spirits are immediately restored by a typical letter from one of his army of loyal fans: 'Dear Big-Head, why don't you . . .' There usually follows an interesting suggestion, which, even if it were physically possible, would not make for 'good radio'.

This grand bunch of ordinary folk, members all of the Terry Wogan Is Tops Society, or TWITS, are the people he relies upon to keep him supplied with a steady torrent of the abuse and contumely which so characterize his Morning Show.

'But what,' I hear you cry, 'is the good of all this? How does it advance man's aspirations, or the Reithian principles of broadcasting?' Shut up a minute, and heed this anonymous letter from a Middlesbrough listener:

'. . . keep up the good work. You are fulfilling a much needed role in society, by being on the receiving end of so much aggression. If it wasn't for you, there would be many more battered grannies . . .'

So there.

In this slim volume you'll find many a ripping yarn of:

The Unspeakable Goings-On at the BBC (our reporter made his excuses, and left)

The DG's Human Sacrifices

The Dance of the BBC Virgins

Wogan's Winners (or how to keep William Hill in the comfort to which he is accustomed)

The Appalling Saga of the Floral Dance ('I thought I could hear the curious moan, of Terence Wogan and a Big Trombone')

Terrible Happenings at Penge-sur-Mer (alors!)

Knickers of World War II

Telling Phrases from the Swahili ('That man is a witch-doctor. He has a frog in his pocket')

plus Hello Chunky, The Nude Vicar, The Beresk Broadcaster . . .

Oh, and many a rattling good verse and finely-honed phrase, I promise you. But you know me, I'd promise you anything to keep you reading.

Frank Dickens, caring nothing for his reputation, did the illustrations.

Who am I?

One hundred listeners, canvassed in the Matlock area, voice their appalling ignorance.

Penge

Set in bracing downland country, Penge-sur-Mer is a blithe little spa, nestling at the foothills of Beckenham, Kent. Penge (pron. PONGE) is a hot-bed of utter respectability, and its denizens dislike my good-natured joshing of the place almost as much as the natives of Gerrards Cross resent it being referred to as 'Gerr-aaards Crorse'.

Ballroom dancing, with all its attendant forbidden pleasures, is rampant in the environs of Penge, thanks to Frank and Peggy Spencer. The major industries are sewing on sequins, and hair-oil. Pamela Adams, Secretary of the Penge (Correct Pronunciation) Society, expands further on some of the local customs.

In Southern Penge
Are chaise-longues
In each front parlour
And busts of Mahler.

In Northern Penge
A pink blancmange
Is de rigueur
For pudding sir.

In Western Penge
It's lemon sponge
For children's parties
Not chips and Smarties.

And Penge East End
They often lend
To camera crews –
Such gorgeous views.

But Penge-sur-Mer
Is still more fair
Your accent's wrong
It's PENGE, not PONGE.

It's funny, but Solihull doesn't much like being described as a 'suburb of Birmingham', either. The following pungent verse, while touching lightly on Penge, and indeed Beckenham, is merely a cover for a slur on my commercial activities . . . God bless them.

I heard you talk on the wireless,
About rich sunken pyramids.
So I sold my villa in Penge-sur-Mer,
And pawned the wife and kids.

Berkley Barclay of Beckenham,
A most delightful chap,
For a mere 10p plus VAT
Sold me a treasure map.

On a dogamaran hired at Barking,
I assembled a motley crew,
And sailed away down the River Thames,
To the Caribbean blue.

We battled on through wind and storm,
Through dysentery and malaria,
Till at last the great day dawned,
We arrived at the treasure area.

All hands scanned the calm blue sea,
Then a shout from the Bosun's daughter,
There just off the old port bow,
Was a cross marked on the water.

Eagerly we dived down deep,
Oh! Lord Sir, we did boob,
No glittering pyramid met our gaze,
Just a tiny red beef cube!

Vic Jarvis,
Forest Hill.

Hello Chunky!

In the beginning was the 'Fight on Flab', a pathetic attempt to hold the flagging interest of the jaded listeners with physical jerks of a violent nature. It has always astonished me that we didn't get a ton of solicitors' letters with every post from listeners who had done themselves a mortal mischief while following my bizarre instructions.

I *did* get a great many letters telling me of strange happenings. A housewife, embarrassed at the prospect of putting her family off their breakfast by lying on the kitchen floor with her legs in the air, repaired to the hall for her contortions, and was somewhat taken aback in the middle of them to see the watery eyes of the postman gazing at her through the letter-box. Many were the tales of being caught *in flagrante delicto* in the bathroom by the window-cleaner, which, in turn, brought heated denials from loyal window-cleaners' wives.

The 'Fight on Flab' became something of a national institution; the BBC even published a book of its esoteric acrobatics. I became the recipient of much hysterical abuse about my own somewhat burly figure, but always stoutly maintained that there was no point at all in Fighting Flab if you didn't have enough blubber to make the battle worthwhile.

Son of the 'Fight on Flab' was 'Hello Chunky!' which was concerned with diets, calories and generally healthful living. It seemed to bring out the poet, the slim-gilt soul that lurks behind every portly exterior:

Now listen 'ere Wogan, you've had your bit of fun,
You've tried to put me off me chips, and lovely sticky bun,
Apart from playing lousy discs, you've set out to depress me,
So let me tell you blue-eyes, your warnings don't impress me.

I'll go on eating trifle, and jam butties by the score,
And home-made scones with cream on, AND THEN I'LL HAVE SOME MORE,
And when they lay me down to rest, and stop me coffin with a cork,
I hope they'll send me on me way, with half a leg of pork.

**Audrey Moss,
Wigan.**

Diana McAdie, a nutritionist who compiled 'Hello Chunky!' for me, suggested that the best way of finding out if you needed to lose weight was to jump up and down, naked, in front of a mirror. If there appeared to be a lot of wobbling and flopping going on, apart from the bits that are designed for that purpose, then diet and exercise were needed.

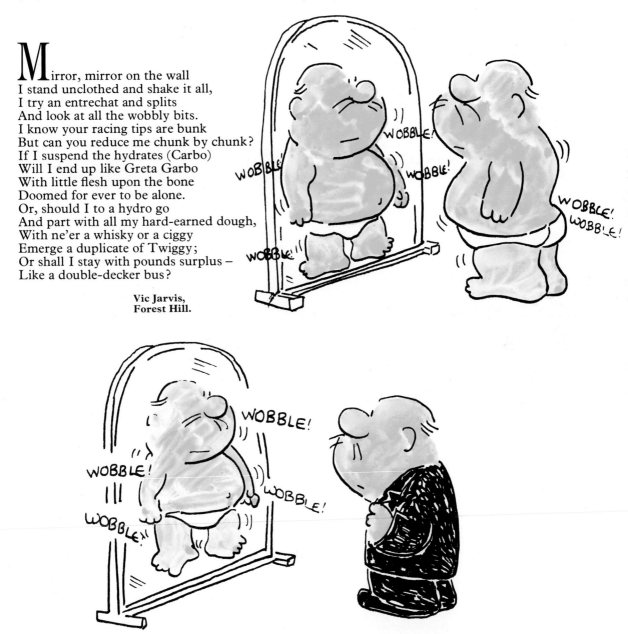

Mirror, mirror on the wall
I stand unclothed and shake it all,
I try an entrechat and splits
And look at all the wobbly bits.
I know your racing tips are bunk
But can you reduce me chunk by chunk?
If I suspend the hydrates (Carbo)
Will I end up like Greta Garbo
With little flesh upon the bone
Doomed for ever to be alone.
Or, should I to a hydro go
And part with all my hard-earned dough,
With ne'er a whisky or a ciggy
Emerge a duplicate of Twiggy;
Or shall I stay with pounds surplus –
Like a double-decker bus?

**Vic Jarvis,
Forest Hill.**

One woman wrote to complain that she had been jumping up and down naked to her heart's content, when her husband had returned home unexpectedly. Getting the wrong end of the stick completely, he immediately tore his clothes off and joined in the homely fun. Now she was pregnant, and what was I going to do about it?

Ode to Chunky

Tried my best to diet,
Even went to gym,
Ran around the local park,
Really tried to slim.
You really are the limit.

Weight and watch are not for me,
One look in the mirror,
Gawd, what do I see.
All my efforts, wasted,
Not a thing has changed.

Only, all the naughty parts,
Have been re-arranged.

E George,
Little Hampden, Bucks.

Kate's Lament

I'm weighing in at ten stone eight,
My clothes are getting tighter,
But as I'm only five foot three
I should be two stones lighter,
I've tried to curb the demon urge
And stop myself from thinking
Of cakes and chocs, lemon drops,
Biscuits, cream, *and* drinking.
The model girls in magazines
Are young, and tall, and slender,
But me, I'm built just like a tank,
With lumps, and bumps, *and* fender.
But then, you see, I'm fifty-three
So I'll just give up hoping,
I'll settle in to middle age
And only give up . . . moping.

Mrs K Bernicky,
Beckenham, Kent

Of Minerals . . .

I heard your strident warning,
On the old steam radio,
Of how we need replacements
When our minerals run low.

I knew I was low in copper,
So I swallowed half a p,
Now I'm a funny shade of green
From a touch of verdigris!

My phosphorous was down a shade,
So I gulped a red-topped match,
And now I have a peculiar itch
In a spot I cannot scratch!

For my calcium deficiency,
I took a stick of chalk,
And now a white line follows me
Everywhere I walk.

For iron I swallowed a few nails,
Now at last I can relax,
But no, the Inland Revenue calls,
They want my 'In Tum Tacks'!

. . . and Vitamins

An SOS I send to you,
I simply know not what to do,
I've lost my lists of Vitamins
And now I'm paying for my sins.

I thought I'd work backwards with Vitamin Z
But all the hair fell off my head.
I didn't do better with Vitamin Y,
Now four-inch lashes cover my eye.

Vitamin X was not better I fear,
There's a dirty great cauli stuck in my ear.
Of Vitamin W the less said the better,
I've more hair on my legs than an Irish Setter.

So Terry, I beg you, implore and insist
Please read out again your Vitamin list
For this fate that has struck me could happen to you
Then what would become of Radio 2?

Vic Jarvis,
Forest Hill.

How the listening audience survived it, must remain a mystery.

Vitas Gerulaitis

My listener and I have had many hours of innocent amusement pouring scorn and detraction on unfortunate singers whose names or appearances lend themselves to the cheap jibe. For instance, Greece's answer to Vera Lynn, Nana Mouskouri, is now firmly entrenched in our minds as Nana Moussaka; the high-toned Barry Manilow is Manly Barrilow; Shirley Bassey has become Burly Chassis. The man who has come in for most of the calumny is Demis Roussos, a large and lovable Cretan who usually appears before an adoring public in a voluminous kaftan. He could scarcely have avoided being called 'The Singing Frock'. Some have even claimed that there's a busy Greek restaurant under the capacious kaftan's folds, and that in quiet moments they can hear merry shouts such as 'Throw another plate on the floor, Demosthenes!' I don't believe it . . . really.

No personality is safe. Comes Wimbledon fortnight and the knives are out for that mysterious tennis-playing disease, Vitas Gerulaitis.

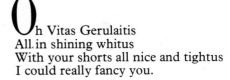

Oh Vitas Gerulaitis
All in shining whitus
With your shorts all nice and tightus
I could really fancy you.

Oh Vitas Gerulaitis
All blond and tanned and brightus
I wish that you'd invite us
To have a game with you.

Oh Vitas Gerulaitis
You're such a lovely sightus
You do it just to spite us
But I could never quite-us
Be really cross with you.

Oh Vitas Gerulaitis
I won't put up a fightus
Come round and have a bitus
And a mug of Aqua Vitas
And I'll get nicely tightus
Andronicus with you.

**Brenda Ray,
Nottingham.**

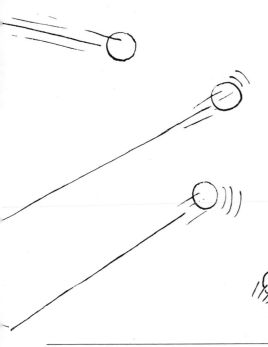

On the Roof

As the first rays of the morning sun bound off All-Souls Church, and strike the bastions of the BBC a resounding blow, a lonely figure, garlanded in thyme and marjoram, and simply but disgustingly clad in string vest, long khaki shorts and scuffed tennis-shoes, lifts his scrawny arms to the sky, and from the BBC's very roof, calls upon the Great God of Broadcasting, Auris, The Ear In The Sky, to aid his minions in another attempt at broadcasting.

Then a wretched, struggling figure, unkempt and dishevelled, is dragged forward, whimpering piteously. He is taken to the very edge of the parapet, and there, the string-vest-clad high priest (or DG, as he is known) strikes the unfortunate victim a resounding blow behind the ear with a wet sock that once belonged to Alvar Liddell. The wretch (or Pete Murray, as he is known) screams in a high-pitched, well-modulated tenor as he falls 200 feet to the street below. As always, a lurking pack of traffic wardens takes the force of the almost-human sacrifice's fall, and Murray limps off to his basement hovel, none the worse for his experience, or as good as he's ever been.

His holy task accomplished, the DG moves across the roof, pausing only occasionally to kick a cringing executive producer, to a broken-down corrugated iron shack (The Home for the Bewildered), there to perform his ablutions and hone his malacca cane for the challenges ahead.

Another day at the BBC has begun.

Later, the roof will come alive with gay, striped awnings and the popping of champagne corks as merry, chattering secretaries and clerks while away the day by the glittering swimming-pool. There is laughter and high-spirited shouting from the tennis courts, and the air is heavy with the scents of jasmine and bougainvillea. The Managing Director (Radio) whistles tunelessly as he tends the DG's vegetable patch, and the Head of Outside Broadcasts polishes the windows with a will.

There are, of course, some Doubting Thomases among my listeners who think that all this is but a figment of my overwrought imagination, who claim that the BBC roof holds nothing more than a flock of down-at-heel pigeons and a producer or two who has been kicked too far upstairs. Tush! if you doubt me, come and see – as these good yeoman listeners have:

Dear Terry,

I represent two families of country yokels from the depths of Derbyshire. One Sunday early in April, complete with dirty wellies and straws from corners of mouth, we came to the big city to show our children the sights. Buckingham Palace, Houses of Parliament, the War Museum and the Tower. But what did our wives insist most on seeing? The BBC, and in particular Terry's Window so that they could in future imagine more realistically the goings-on so beautifully described.

So we stood at the top of Regent Street and gazed in wonder at those magnificent bulwarks of the BBC. So this was where the great master talked to us from. By astute use of our divining rod, sense of smell and allowing for the wind, we even worked out the window you view from. So there were the edifices of Regent Street and the hole in the road where David Hamilton landed on his head. So there was the DG's garden (aren't his shallots early this year?).

But other questions remained unanswered. Can you help?
1 Was the person with the mop and cigarette in reception the DG herself?
2 Was the other lady in reception, wearing a dressing gown being frantically chased by a man in pinstripes, rehearsing for the Moscow Olympics?
3 Are the BBC bike sheds those premises under Oxford Circus with the sign of a red circle and horizontal line?

John Caws,
Boylestone, Derbyshire.

In answer to those thought-provoking queries:
1 No. The Chairman.
2 No. It was a member of the BBC Board of Governors, jogging with Lord Longford.
3 No. That is the DG's private bunker, in the likely event of a coup d'état.

Great British Food

When all a body has time for, of an early morn, is a gulp of coffee and a swig of almost-natural orange juice, you can scarcely blame him indulging in food fantasies as the pangs of hunger gnaw at his very vitals.

So, at breakfast time, my listeners help themselves from sideboards groaning under the weight of silver dishes full of kedgeree, kidneys, bacon (albeit not as crispy as it was before the war), eggs done every conceivable way, chipolatas, the odd chop, and bowls of steaming porridge.

As the old brain becomes increasingly addled, I forget how the great 'Porridge on the Gallop' controversy started. Enough to say that someone was sufficiently foolish to state that in the Great Houses of England, Milord of the Manor always took his porridge at a brisk trot around the baronial hall, and only a scurvy knave or, indeed, a varlet, would dream of sitting down to eat the stuff.

Dear Mr Wogan,

Now the 'Porridge on the Gallop' controversy has once again raised its ugly head, I feel I must settle the matter once and for all. The tradition has its roots in early Scottish history when the laird would take two of his gillies and head for the haggis hills. This being in the days before battery haggis breeding methods. The porridge was actually bait for the haggis, but the journey often being very long the laird would tear off a piece of porridge, cover it with salt in an attempt to kill the taste and chew it as they went along. When they got to the hills the gillies would lay the bait, and when the haggis came down to nibble the porridge the laird would creep up behind the unsuspecting haggis and hit it between the gillies, usually using a No 7 spurtle. The haggis would remain on its back thrashing its legs in the air until it was gathered up and taken back to the castle to be fattened up, only to be slaughtered on Burns night.

If your laughter is truly due to your jeans, I suggest you buy a larger pair or broadcast standing up.

Lord Ferendune
Lechlade, Gloucestershire.

This kind of stuff naturally led to many a boring old Scots tale of how the honest gillie would boil 100 cwt of porridge every Sunday, and leave it to cool in a bedroom drawer.

Then, every morning, before departing up the side of Ben Nevis after the sheep, he would hack out a lump of cold porridge to sustain him through the blizzards.

Then people started sending me strange, heathen artefacts carved from wood, called 'postles'.

The Postle

Porridge is stirred with a postle,
You funny old Irish loon,
Sure, even out in the backwoods,
They've heard of a postle spoon.

'Tis made from the horns of a haggis,
Carved and polished to taste,
And worn to the left of the sporran,
That's just below the waist.

It's also used in the Highlands,
To remove the dumplings from stew,
And at night is tucked in a bedsock,
Along with the old Skean Dhu.

Sometimes down in the Lowlands,
They wear them strapped to their legs,
And use them each Passion Sunday,
To shell their new-laid scotch eggs.

I know this is all authentic,
I was told by a couple of swells,
Namely Brenda of Brixton,
And 'Disgusted', Tunbridge Wells!

**Vic Jarvis,
Forest Hill.**

And, of course, it was only a matter of time until I received a stave or two in praise of another great British delicacy: tripe.

Tripe

You can braise it in sauterne
In a great big Grecian Urn,
You can hang it till it's blue
And slap it in a stew,
You can fluff it, you can stuff it,
You can fry in fat and puff it
Oh tripe is the stuff for me.

You can mash it, you can hash it,
You can whip it up and smash it,
You can drop it on the floor,
It'll still come back for more.
Yes, tripe is the stuff for me.
For it takes a lot of beating,
Forgive me for repeating,
Yes, tripe is the stuff for me.

**Brenda Ray,
Nottingham.**

Considering how I had pushed the kindly folk of Cornwall beyond human endurance with my rendition of their 'Floral Dance', it now seems an extraordinarily plucky, nay foolhardy, move to have broadcast 'live' from Penzance. But I did, and anyway most of the smaller bruises have now virtually disappeared. It was a wonderful morning – the seagulls cried, the people were jolly, I ate fresh crab claws, and a baker presented me with a four-foot-long, two-foot-wide, genuine Cornish Pasty. We carried the wonderful-smelling, steaming giant to the Radio Car, in order to attack it with a blunt instrument after the programme. Then 'live', on the air, the great Pasty slid off a table, and covered the interior of the van to a depth of four feet in meat, potatoes and gravy. Two years later, they're still finding bits of it in the equipment . . .

Cornish Calamity

'Wogan's coming,' the Cornish cried,
'All our maidens we must hide.'
'The ladies adore him,' the fishermen said,
'What about sending him a mackerel head?'
'Don't 'ee be so cruel,' came the baker's voice,
'We'll treat the man to something choice.
A pasty we'll make, an 'andsome one,
Get out the chuck steak, 'tatoes, onion,
His initials we'll place on the crisp brown crust,
To show in Radio 2 we trust.'

But Oh! as in the car he sped
The pasty broke, Terry turned his head
'A beautiful one, 'twas grand,' he wept
As deftly away from the gravy he leapt.
So beware all you who bake pasties grand,
Then give them to folks from Ireland,
Pack them secure in a leak-proof box
To prevent hot gravy dripping into their socks!

Mrs Thelma Morgan,
Farnham,
Surrey (but a Cornish exile).

'Set a spell, and let your saddle cool'

Not many people know that I was probably the only boy in my native township of Limerick to have a personally autographed photo of Gene Autry aboard Champion, the Wonder Horse. I never went much on Roy Rogers and Trigger, maybe it was the way his eyeballs disappeared into his forehead whenever he smiled. Gene seemed the straighter shooter somehow.

So it seems that I've always been steeped in prairie lore, and songs of the sagebrush. I've seen enough of the cowboy epics to survive the Mojave Desert with just the odd prickly pear cactus, and I daresay that I could recognize an Apache war-arrow if I saw it sticking out of Ward Bond's back. Incidentally, that reminds me of one of the most sophisticated yet barbaric means of easing the BBC's Block in Promotion – the 'Run of the Arrow'. The DG would loose a shaft from his longbow in the direction of Oxford Circus, and from wherever the arrow landed, an unfortunate senior executive would be given a head start. If he made it down Regent Street to Piccadilly Circus before the whooping horde of junior bucks caught up with him, he kept his job, and his scalp. If not . . . Songs like 'Git Along Little Dogies' and 'Empty Saddles in the Old Corral' are meat and drink to me, so it's natural that my radio programme should have the tang of the camp-fire and the sniff of the bunkhouse about it. At least that's what we put it down to.

A cat called Wogan

PURR!
PURR!
PURR!

Standing at stud, in some lush pasture, is a bull called Wogan. A prize-winning St Bernard and a Wolfhound bear the same proud name. Recently, a listener named a couple of kids after me – I was a bit nonplussed when they turned out to be *goats*.

Dear Terry,

Heard you say the other morning that you'd had a couple of goats named after you. My son Kenton is an avid listener to your programme whilst milking the cows. Consequently we now have a cow named Terry Wogan. Incidentally you are a very good milker.

Stan Honeybun,
Glastonbury, Somerset.

An unfortunate thoroughbred racehorse (of which fine animal, more later) was lumbered with a similar burden. And then the cat-lovers got me.

Dear Terrible Wogan,

I heard you read out a letter this morning from a listener concerning his cat's name, and how he wouldn't let his mother call it Wogan . . . Well we HAVE called ours Wogan, and I know you will be riveted to your BBC stool to hear why we chose such a strange name. Like all good fairy stories it starts : Once upon a time . . . My husband, who incidentally is called Terry, said that he was adamant he was not going to have a cat, so when we decided to get one we thought we should call it Wogan. This is because he hates cats with the same intensity that he hates you, and thought that every time he kicked it across the room he could shout 'Wogan' and would feel a lot better.

As it turned out it was a very good choice as he (the cat, not my husband, though come to think of it) has your same rotund middle, bright yellow eyes and bushy tail, though his is striped. He also talks non-stop first thing in the morning when he wants food. If you bring home rats, mice and rabbits for breakfast, then it surely is a family trait, but what about lying on your back rolling over waiting to have a fuss made of you . . . it wouldn't surprise me. I know you will think this all a load of Old Wogan, but you only have to ring up the cat's vet, or the kennels where he spent his two weeks' summer holiday.

We call him Wogie or Woges for short . . . my husband calls him Rat.

**Vivien L Hart,
Ashford, Kent.**

The Floral Dance

It was at an impressionable age that I first heard my father, Lord Wogan of the Reeks, intone the 'Cornish Floral Dance'. He would make the welkin ring with it for a radius of 10 miles as he performed his ablutions of a morning. My father had other crowd-pleasers in his repertoire, such as 'Dead for Bread', but the Floral Dance remained etched in my memory, and probably stunted my growth.

So, when the opportunity came to have my revenge on the thing, I grasped it. I'm only sorry that so many music-lovers had to suffer in the process.

Almost as soon as I began playing the instrumental version of the aforementioned Cornish Disease, by the Faggots and Gastric Brass and Reed Ensemble, or, as they prefer to be known, the Brighouse and Rastrick Band, I was reminded of my boyhood suffering, and it was an automatic reflex to mumble along with it.

The instrumental version subsequently became a ginormous hit, selling well over a million copies, but I received even more disgruntled letters than usual, from people who had heard the record on my programme, rushed out in a panic, bought it, and then found that I wasn't singing on it!

Being as quick as your other men to know a hot property when they heard it, the record companies paid absolutely no attention.

Then a trusting, if ageing, singer/producer called Mike Redway had the idea of doing a vocal version with our hero. Well, my bird (as they say in Cornwall), you know all too well the rest of the unsavoury tale:

How a hitherto discerning public actually bought the thing, and made it into a hit, rising to No 15 in the Top Twenty.

How this unexpected disaster provoked not one, but *two* appearances on 'Top of the Pops' by a paunchy, raddled old disc-jockey.

How, in an effort to placate the angry weenies, punks, teds and teenies, this pathetic figure hurled flowers at them.

How they hurled them back, shouting 'Get off, you silly old fool,' and other youthful jibes, with which I will not trouble you.

It's not surprising really that the more sensitive poetically-minded souls took it so badly:

D ear Terry,

On the advice of a friend, I recently
bought your recording of 'The Floral Dance',
and on playing the record,
I thought I heard the curious tone,
Of Wogan on the gramophone,
Grunting here, and groaning there,
Devoid of timing, tone and flair,
Trying to make the most of his chance,
With his hideous attempt at 'The Floral Dance'.

John Betteley,
Birmingham.

Floral Tribute

I thought I could hear the curious moan
Of Terence Wogan and a big trombone,
Even though he wasn't dumb
He got drunk on a tot of rum.
When drunk in a trance
He began to sing the Floral Dance.

As I was made deaf on a winter's night
Stars were dark in the darkened light,
Then he rode off upon his mare
Into the foul and dampened air,
Of that quaint old studio.

Borne from a far Thames River breeze
Joining the smell of Terry's knees
Distant moans of an old man's voice
Played by a DJ recorder by chance
And a bomb came floating down.

That put an end to the curious moan
Of Terence Wogan and a big trombone
Even though he wasn't dumb
He got drunk on a tot of rum.
When he was drunk in a trance
He began to sing the Floral Dance,
He began to sing the Floral Dance.

Anon.

Terry and his Floral Dance

I hurried down at a quarter to eight, turned on the radio to keep a date,
Started the breakfast, had to frown, there was not a single sound,
In our quaint, old-fashioned town.

I hit it on the back, 'punched it up the throat', could not get a
Solitary note,
Spilled the milk, burned the toast, made them all late 'cause I was slow,
But I had to get that set to go, FOR

I listen to the man with the curious tone with a voice as mellow as a big trombone,
Gave the set a poke with my thumb but not so much as a rum-tum-tum,
Today there would be no chance of my daily session with the Floral Dance.

I felt so lonely standing there but I could only stand and stare,
Has Terry got up the DG's 'snout'? Has the DG driven him out
Of quaint old London town?

Then I thought tomorrow he's bound to be back – if the DG has not given
Him the sack –
With outstretched hands he'll rush along, down Regent Street amid the throng
And burst into his jolly song. And he'll

Sing like a man with the curious tone with a voice as mellow as a big
trombone
No need to poke the set with my thumb for he will be there with a rum-tum-tum
Then we all can sing and prance to the merry music of the Floral Dance.

Dancing here, jigging there, Weetybangs flying everywhere,
I will be in my normal, happy trance,
HURRAY FOR TERRY AND HIS FLORAL DANCE.

Barbara Thompson.

Dear Mr Wogan

Is that your real name or like the other recording superstars is it just to obscure the fact that you were born Stanley Trench? Anyway, I've always liked your chocolates and towelling and as a mark of my appreciation I am sending you a lyric for your follow-up waxing. You'll see that it fits the Floral Dance, which seems to be the only tune you know.

Keith Hamnett,
Altrincham, Cheshire.

The Floral Dance

Chorus
Ho, ho, the Terry Wogan Show
Half past seven and it's off we go
Tips and quips, music so to speak
All together all five days are weak.

Low Bit No 1
Every morning on the radio
Why not listen to the Terry Wogan Show
Something for everybody every day
Specially when he goes on holiday
Ho ho ho ho ho ho ho ho

Low Bit No 2
If you like listening to a certain song
Don't tell Terry Wogan or he'll sing along
There are times when he tries to sing the Floral Dance
Other times the music stands a chance
Ho ho ho ho ho ho ho ho.

Knickers of World War 2

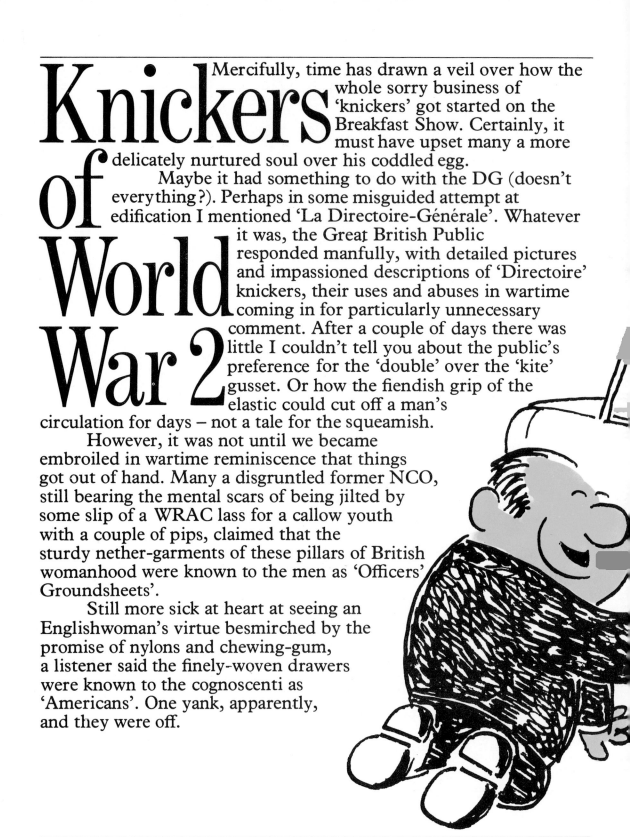

Mercifully, time has drawn a veil over how the whole sorry business of 'knickers' got started on the Breakfast Show. Certainly, it must have upset many a more delicately nurtured soul over his coddled egg.

Maybe it had something to do with the DG (doesn't everything?). Perhaps in some misguided attempt at edification I mentioned 'La Directoire-Générale'. Whatever it was, the Great British Public responded manfully, with detailed pictures and impassioned descriptions of 'Directoire' knickers, their uses and abuses in wartime coming in for particularly unnecessary comment. After a couple of days there was little I couldn't tell you about the public's preference for the 'double' over the 'kite' gusset. Or how the fiendish grip of the elastic could cut off a man's circulation for days – not a tale for the squeamish.

However, it was not until we became embroiled in wartime reminiscence that things got out of hand. Many a disgruntled former NCO, still bearing the mental scars of being jilted by some slip of a WRAC lass for a callow youth with a couple of pips, claimed that the sturdy nether-garments of these pillars of British womanhood were known to the men as 'Officers' Groundsheets'.

Still more sick at heart at seeing an Englishwoman's virtue besmirched by the promise of nylons and chewing-gum, a listener said the finely-woven drawers were known to the cognoscenti as 'Americans'. One yank, apparently, and they were off.

The nastiest calumny of all, however, on a garment that played a vital role in the war effort, was the nickname 'Messerschmitt'. These, you may correctly imagine, came down without a fight.

After all that, it was no surprise to me when the directive from above arrived on my desk. Its message was succinct. 'Drop the knickers!' was all it said.

Spring has sprung

Of all the seasons, Spring brings out the worst in my listeners. Something to do with the 'sap', as they like to call me:

I t was an April morning, and the rain was falling fast;
And Spring was in the air, as you could tell by the icy blast.
The daffodils were wincing, and the birds were all off-key,
But I tried hard to be cheerful, and the brighter side to see.
'At least,' I said, 'It's done its worst; it just can't get more black.'
Then Wogan started his programme, and I had to take it back.

Joan Wells,
Benfleet, Essex.

A regular little ray of sunshine, even on the dullest day, that's me.

During the *Times* newspaper stoppage, I boldly put myself forward as a 'surrogate' Letters Column for those who were feeling the need to let it all hang out in the old Thunderer. I am still picking letters about the First Cuckoo out of my hair. This, of course, provoked a lot of unkind stuff about being able to hear a cuckoo anytime between the hours of 7.30 and 10.00 in the mornings, on Radio 2.

Harry Hartill takes it all with the phlegmatic calm of that put-upon breed, the Traffic Warden. I wish we had a few more like him around the Broadcasting House meters:

I SAID 'DID YOU HEAR THE FIRST CUCKOO'?

Spring Fever

The joys of spring, my
Heart stands still.
The cuckoo, lamb, and
Pneumatic drill.

The coned off lanes, the
Diversion signs,
The Traffic Wardens, and
Yellow lines.

The half dug hole, wet
Tar and fog,
The flattened hedgehog,
The straying dog.

The jack-knifed tanker, the
Straying sheep.
The abnormal loads, behind
Which we creep.

The police car siren, the
Radar trap,
The breakdown call, the
Waiting nap.

Road licence, tax and
MOT,
These joys of Spring wait
You and me.

Harry Hartill.

Spring at the BBC is a time of new growth, bustle and vigour. Fresh faces, as yet unacquainted with the 'Block in Promotion', new ideas not yet trampled into the dust – even a Radio 3 producer sometimes comes up with an idea! Executives, shaking off the dust of hibernation, begin their childish, harmless clamour for a new carpet. Occasionally, an over-enthusiastic young clerk who has broken the Rules of the Lord by, say, complaining about the switchboard ladies, is found lying senseless and battered in some corridor. Generally, though, cheery bonhomie prevails, and nowhere more so than on the greensward of the BBC roof.

There, every Thursday in spring, come rain or shine, is held the historic and strangely moving 'Dance of the Virgins'. The origins of this mysterious rite are, of course, long lost in the mists of time. But the biggest mystery of all remains: why does nobody ever turn up for the thing?

I will gratefully leave the subject where it lies, with this sturdy little offering, again from Joan Wells:

That time of year has come again
When we must alter all the clocks,
Unstitch the winter underwear
And wash the piles of dirty socks.
It is the time, the jolly time
When all the kids get chickenpox,
And when you've settled all the bills
Your bank account is on the rocks.
But it is spring, so let us sing
Hey ho, and jolly hollyhocks;
Hail (also snow, and fog, and sleet)
The merry vernal equinox.

Songs for Swingers

'Songs for Swinging . . .' is an idea as old as time, or Acker Bilk. It was that scrumpy-loving rascal who gave me the idea, as we journeyed together to the fair town of Castlebar, in the West of Ireland, for the annual International Song Contest. Acker had a million examples of Swinging Songs, garnered over the years by his merry Paramount Jazz Band, and when I mentioned it over the air, in a moment of passing weakness, I found that everyone else in the country had a million of 'em as well. I don't think anything on the programme before or since has promoted such a volume of mail. Herewith, from the thousands, some telling examples of the genre:

Songs for Swinging Homicidal Maniacs:
'When you grow too old to scream
I'll have you to dismember.'

Songs for Swinging Doctors:
'Isn't it Rheumatic'
'Let's Cut the Whole Thing Off'
'A Pretty Girl is like a Malady'.

Songs for Swinging Silicone Manufacturers:
'Mammaries are Made of This'.

Songs for Swinging Monarchs:
'Might as well Reign until September'
'Kings Ain't What They Used to be'.

Songs for Swinging Wrestlers:
'As Long as He Knees Me'
'I've Got You under My Shin'.

Songs for Swinging Perverts:
'Never Smile at a Paedophile'
'Doin' What Comes Unnaturally'.

Songs for Swinging Amateur Photographers:
'Someday My Prints Will Come'.

Songs for Swinging Sewer Men:
'You Stepped out of a Drain'
'Great Falls of Mire'.

Songs for Swinging Magistrates:
'Someday I'll Fine You'.

Songs for Swinging Dentists:
'Decay We Were'
'Gummy the Moonlight'
'Plaque in the Old Routine'.

Songs for Swinging Drunks:
'The Soaks who Live on the Hill'.

Songs for Swinging Knights:
'I Could Have Lanced All Night'.

Songs for Swinging Antique Dealers:
'Just One of Those Mings'.

Songs for Swinging Arabs:
'The Shriek of Agony'.

Songs for Swinging Murderers:
'Stranglers in the Night'.

Songs for Swinging Bed Bugs:
'On the Sheet Where You Live'.

Songs for Swinging Ornithologists:
'Give Me Five Linnets More'
'Boiled Beef and Parrots'.

Songs for Swinging Londoners:
'I Get a Kick out of Kew'
'Putney Among the Girls'
'What Kind of Fulham I?'
'Hendoneath the Arches'
'Harrow Young Lovers'
'Wembley Red Red Robin
Comes Bob, Bob, Bobbin Along'.

Songs for Swinging Nuns:
'I Left My Heart with Some Franciscans'.

Songs for Swinging Bakers:
'Kiss Me Buns and Kiss Me Pies
and Kiss Me Buns Again'
'I Get a Cake Out of You'.

Songs for Swinging Eunuchs:
'I Can't Give You Anything But Laughs, Baby'.

Songs for Swinging German Gays: 'You Need Hans'.

Songs for Swinging German Asylum Doctors:
'God Rest Ye Jerry Mentalmen'.

Songs for Swinging Cricketers:
'Amazing W G Grace'.

Songs for Swinging Longbow Manufacturers:
'I've Got Yew Under My Skin'.

Songs for Swinging Oyster Fishermen:
'Has Anybody Seen My Pearl?'

Songs for Swinging Bookworms:
'Paperback Biter'.

Songs for Swinging Undertakers:
'Painting the Shrouds with Sunshine'.

**Contributions from Francis Lamb, London E6;
Bob and Barbara Ross, Cyffylliog, Clwyd;
Rosemary Gilbert, Andover, Hampshire;
O H Thomas, Malvern, Worcestershire;
David Snell, Tillingham, Essex; Lorna Parkins,
Streatham, London; Wug Plumb and Rosie Jarbo,
Worcester; H W (Lon) Chaney, Ickenham,
Middlesex; Edith Mateer, Twickenham, Middlesex.**

...AND KICK!
... AND KICK!

Jimmy Young

As you will know from reading the lives of other great stars, it's a Lonely Life At The Top. Picture, if you will, the great disc-jockey: a solitary figure, hunched over his microphone, engrossed in the fine art of communicating his thoughts to millions of listeners, avid as they are for his every word, smiling at his nuances, chuckling heartily as the *bons mots* trip off his sensitive lips. A man, you would say, at the Top of the Tree, with the World at his Feet. A social lion, you would aver, with wet-lipped lovelies catering for his every whim, the rich and famous beating paths to his door.

THE SCREENS! Yes, but it's not *all* fun being Jimmy Young . . . It can be lonely too – pathetic, even.

HIM— Sometimes, of a morning, I feel a surge of pity as the nurse wheels the grand old broadcaster into my studio in his bath-chair, and after wetting his dry, cracked lips with a sponge, we get a
OLOGY few weak, rambling sentences from him. Often the cry goes up: 'Nurse! The screens!' But it's usually too late. Hard to believe that this shattered husk was once the Singing Baker's Boy, The Man From Laramie, the one who was Too Young, the Donny Osmond of his day.

EVER HEARD I never show him the letters, of course. For they
OF HER would surely break the old chap's heart. How can people be so horrid?

'When are they going to put Jimmy Young out of his misery?'
'Wouldn't it be *kinder* to have him shot?'
Sometimes, they *even* criticize *me*:
'Why don't you two get married?'
'What's the matter, is he your father or something?'
Cruel, cruel world! There, there, Jimbo . . .

Give the boy a Goldfish

Perish the thought that all that ever comes an honest broadcaster's way from his doughty band of listeners is but dog's abuse and the discouraging word. There was, for instance, a wonderful woman called Lady Angela who followed my every move in a Volkswagen bus, which she dubbed the 'Wogan Wagon'. It was plastered with photos and posters of our mutual idol, and wherever I went, be it to open a fete or close down a supermarket, there would be the 'Wogan Wagon' with Lady Angela and a band of young people she had bribed heavily to come along and cheer on the ageing funster with word and gesture.

Lady Angela turned up at the dingy portals of the BBC, on birthdays and anniversaries, bearing crates of champagne, bouquets of flowers and cakes moulded into the shape of gramophones. If I attempted to refuse the largesse she became hurt and angered, and when I tried to thank her she blushed and ran. Lovely, generous woman. I've often wondered if she just felt sorry for me. Other listeners remember my family's birthdays and anniversaries better than I do. Indeed, when my mother was in hospital some years ago, a couple of listeners, hearing me read out a request for her, sent my *mother* cards and gifts!

Listeners send cheques and money to my 'starving' children at Christmas and birthday time, which naturally I return, if possible, with thanks, or else send on to the BBC Charities office.

I get eggs at Easter, shamrock on St Patrick's Day, primroses on Primrose Day, roses on St George's Day, 'Fisherman's Friend' lozenges when I'm wheezy, toys, ties, socks, pet rocks, sweets and Smurfs. I get bits of cake from weddings, and haggis for no good reason whatsoever.

A few years ago, a goldfish which my children had won at a fair passed away to the sounds of great weeping, wailing and the gnashing of milk teeth. Believing, as I do, that I should hold nothing back from my listeners, I bruited the sad news abroad. Two days later, I was the recipient of a polythene bag full of water and a dozen goldfish! I proudly carried them to Paddington and we all took the train home. The eldest survivor died only last year. Do you think if I said the ashtrays in my wife's Ferrari were full . . .?

DEAR TERRY.
 SORRY TO HEAR YOU
LOST YOUR GOLDFISH.
I AM SENDING...

'Can they smell us from here?' Occasionally, in a vain attempt to revitalize the jaded listener, I will refer to my 'bronicals' being stuffed, or my 'various' veins causing me agony. Sometimes of an early morn, goaded beyond endurance by thirst, I will shriek that unless some passing Samaritan gets me a cup of coffee, I will assuredly go beresk. Now, you would imagine that this piteous whingeing, if not provoking waves of sympathy, would at least bring a trickle of condolence. Instead the letters pour in, pointing out my appalling ignorance.

Dear Sir,
The word you are searching for is 'berserk', which I believe has its roots in unseemly behaviour by the Norse. Still, being Irish, I suppose you couldn't be expected to know these things . . .'

I have been known to slip in the odd Latin tag, with the passing Classical scholar in mind. 'Sic transit Gloria Swanson,' I intone, hoping for a scholarly reaction. So far – zilch. If he's out there, he's not with me. Probably a Radio 1 man.

Hoping to snag the ear of the sleeping Celt, I slip easily into my native Erse: 'Tá sé mahogany gaspipe!' (Give the woman in the bed more porther!) No answer, comes the stern reply.

Yet, one word of French – a 'phrase utile' to help the 'O' levels along, and I'm up to my oxters in:

Everyday French: 'Avez-vous de jupes-culottes?' (Have you any cami-knickers?)

French Pronunciation Simplified: Toto: Good day, my uncle. I to-you wish a good and happy year. Mamma to-me has said that if you to-me give a sovereign, I am-to take well care to not it lose . . .'

A passing piece of South African 'kwela' music, played if I'm not mistaken on the old nose-flute and called 'Tom Hark', followed by a hearty 'Jambo!' to calm the natives, produced from a demented old Africa hand a Swahili phrase book, full of such pithy pars as: 'That man is a witch-doctor. He has a frog in his pocket.' This was immediately followed by a letter from Sheila Thomas containing some more beauties of the bush, kloof and veldt.

Dear Terry Wogan,

Hearing your African interlude this morning re 'Tom Hark' etc., reminded me of an incident which happened a couple of years ago.

There was great excitement in the parish when we heard that an African Minister from Uganda was to visit the Vicarage for a month. The Vicar appealed for offers of help to entertain him as he wanted to sample life with a typical English family. Being more 'typical' than most, we offered to have him to stay for a weekend. As the Vicar wasn't sure whether or not he spoke English we borrowed an English–Swahili phrase book from someone who had spent several years in Uganda. The phrases had us nearly helpless with laughter.

Examples:
Do not expectorate about here!
Usiteme mate huku!

Put in the rubble and beat it well.
Tia kokoto kapigilie sana.
Can they smell us from here?
Watapata kutuona kutoka hapa?
Split the skull and give the brains to the cook.
Pasua kichwa koripe mpishi ule ubongo.
How old are these droppings?
Mavi haya ya lini?
The white ants have eaten the timbers.
Miti yake imeliwa na mehwa.
A snake has bitten me.
Nimeumwa na nyoka.

Needless to say, when he arrived he spoke faultless English, lived in a bungalow with colour TV and every mod. con. and the nearest he had been to a lion or tiger was at the National Game Reserve Park near Kampala. He couldn't understand Swahili and said his native language was Luandan.

**Sheila M Thomas,
Rossendale,
Lancashire.**

MAKE YOURSELF AT HOME

As we used to say in Ireland when I was a lad: 'Póg mo thóin!' And if you think I'm going to translate *that* . . .

The haunted fish tank

I am, by nature, placid. Boring, even. The fiery Celtic blood that ought to course through my veins appears to have diluted. Only rarely do my eyes start from my head, and flecks of foam appear on my chiselled lips. That occurs when people say things like:

'Put your name there. I can't stand you myself, but it's for my daughter.'

'Only $2\frac{1}{2}$ hours work a day, eh? Not bad.'

'You Irish – such wonderful talkers.'

'Golf is basically a simple game.'

'I never watch television, myself.'

I watch it all the time, and I don't care who knows it. Whenever I'm in the States, I have it with my wheatybangs for breakfast. I watch television for amusement and relaxation. If any information or education happens to slip through while my brain is resting, fine. So I often refer to whatever epic I've been watching on the 'haunted fish tank' the night before. I may pass comment on Kate Jackson's astounding acting in 'Charlie's Angels', or on Petrocelli's tardiness in building his house, a task he appears to have been at for ever, but which is still barely past the foundations. Listeners quickly riposte that even if the raunchy young lawyer does get it up, since he appears to be building it down a gulch in the middle of the New Mexico Desert, his chances of mains drainage are limited!

Nothing appears to infuriate the viewing public more than the amount of good food that goes to waste in the average American pot-boiler. Jim Rockford is for ever putting down his tacos untasted; but the worst offenders in this respect are the denizens of 'Dallas'. Nearly all the action in this simple tale of

prairie folk takes place over breakfast, lunch and dinner. But not a drop of orange juice nor a sliver of prime Texas beef ever passes the lips of old Jock, Miss Ellie, Bobby, Pammy, JR, Sue-Ellen, or little Lucy.

Plenty more passes their lips though, most of it of stunning banality, in this hairy tale of sin, sex and skullduggery 'neath Western skies. All this in the very locale where heretofore never was heard a discouragin' word. Certainly no television series has ever provoked more reaction from my listeners – particularly the dyed-in-the-wool villain of the piece, the heinous JR.

Dear Terry,
Re that swine JR Ewing. I'm amazed that someone hasn't stuffed him down one of his own oil wells. You say you feel sorry for Bobby – well you must be daft. Pammy's right, those Ewings are all the same. After all, Bobby knows what JR's been up to and yet he expects Pammy to return to South Fork. Could you bear to sit at the same dinner table as that creep under Pammy's circumstances. Of course you couldn't – you hate the man and you haven't even met him. His sickly smile and Texan drawl is enough to put anybody off their food.

About Lucy. She's not a dwarf at all. The other women are as big as their men, so I would guess that they're probably six-footers. Lucy is average height. She's supposed to be seventeen by the way, NOT fifteen as you seem to think.

June Thompson,
Lincoln.

The aforementioned Lucy, 17 going on 47, became known to me and mine as 'The Poison Dwarf' or 'Bridget the Midget', but she was not without her followers:

Dear Mr Wogan,
Re 'DALLAS'
Let us cease all this endless chatter about JR and aim for fair play for 'The Midget.' One can hardly fail to notice her lack of opportunity to display her talent as an actress. Her anatomy we *all* know about but this week her ever-diminishing lines of dialogue were reduced to one word, 'Pam,' which she uttered when things looked bad during the trial scene. Now Charlene (as is her real name) gave the line all she's got, which is quite considerable, but surely she deserves better than this.

By the way, is it my imagination but does JR don his safari jacket when he is about to stoop to even more evil depths.

John Leigh,
Gwernaffield, Clwyd.

Not everybody watched 'Dallas', of course:

Dear Terry,
   What's all this rubbish I hear every morn
About 'Dallas' and 'JR' (some American corn).

Not a programme I watch 'cause each Tuesday at eight
I go to the pub for a drink with my mate.

But then for two weeks I watched 'Call My Bluff'
(Cause Roy Marsden was on – and he's lovely stuff)

And between 'Call My Bluff' and 'Blake's Seven' I saw
This programme 'Dallas' which causes such a furore.

Now I readily admit that JR is not nice
And the programme is riddled with intrigue and vice

But surely a man of your standing and brain
Can find better causes for a campaign.

How about a petition demanding that we
Have more manly programmes to watch on TV.

Bring back 'Z Cars' and 'Warship' and series like that
Not American soap opera with a JR-type rat.

Jim Rockford, he's manly and you liked him before
The nasty in 'Dallas' became such a bore.

There's that nice Mr Telford who's hit a bad patch
Compared to his troubles the Dwarf is no match.

How about it TW, wish 'Dallas' afar,
And let's hear no more of that rotter JR.

Denise Hulme,
Stoke-on-Trent.

But those that did, took it seriously:

THEY CAN'T BE REALLY
ENJOYING THOSE STEAKS...
THEY ARE ONLY EATING
THEM ONE AT A TIME...

Dear Terry,

Surely there must be some deep psychological reason for this devil JR's behaviour. Perhaps he was left with only six servants in that huge house with gale-force winds blowing around it when he was three months old, or was deprived of his gold-handled dummy when he was ten. That beautiful Bobby, how does he manage to keep his hands off JR, he's even too good to realize what's in it for him. It's not surprising they are all ga-ga living in such confined quarters with Big Daddy's eye upon them. He doesn't see much, does he!

Why do we keep watching? Well, it's a bit like listening to you Terry, one day it will all make sense and it's always good for a laugh or a gnashing of teeth in the meantime.

Cheers for now, I'm off to the dentist for a bit more punishment.

Irene Robson,
Letchworth, Hertfordshire.

It is important of course, to get the historical background to the whole sorry mess:

Dear Terry,
I'm just writing to let you know that you do in fact have five listeners as my wife and I listen to your programme every day, and up to now we've remained anonymous, but following your comments on Wednesday about nobody actually eating in the 'Rockford Files', I felt I had to write and correct you as this is the first time I've heard you misleading your listeners and now wonder whether you do in fact watch these programmes as I definitely saw Jimbo tucking into a Yorkshire pudding and Rocky also had a big mouthful of the sandwiches that he'd made earlier on.
While I'm on the subject, I thought you'd like to know a few facts about 'Dallas' which no one has yet brought to light.
Miss Elly was in fact Elly May Clampet before she married Jock and when her Pa (Jed) and the family died after eating possum pie which had gone off, she inherited the oil empire. She met Jock after he'd got well and truly cheesed off with being beaten up by John Wayne every time he made a Western film with him. JR's earlier days were taken up with making the early Donald Duck cartoons and then later he was the Penguin in 'Batman', have you noticed how he has still retained the special walk from those experiences.
And have you noticed how Pamela's Blankety Blanks have doubled in size since she changed her hairstyle.
Anyway, why don't you get JR to guest on 'Blankety Blank' then you could stab him in the eye with your microphone on behalf of all your fans.

**Julius Wyszogrodzki,
Carlisle.**

However, while myself and the rest of the loonies sat transfixed of a Tuesday night by the sight of Jock sprinkling sugar on his eggs (no wonder he never ate them), or the rest of the cast shivering by the swimming pool in a Force 9 gale, more uplifting things were afoot on BBC 1, viz:

Ode to David Attenborough

I'm a fan of David Attenborough; he beats 'Dallas' on TV,
The private lives of animals are popular you see.

Now if you watch his programme it's the way they reproduce
That makes animals so popular so let me introduce

The Viewer's simple guide to the wildlife mating habits.
I'll include as many as I can but I promise not to mention rabbits.

In the everglades you can observe the sex life of a bullfrog.
Perhaps you'll think it noisy but less painful than the hedgehog.

The mating of an electric eel is something that will shock
And when two elephants make love the jungle starts to rock.

To the African hyena it's not a laughing matter.
The armadillos do it with a rattle and a clatter.

Hippos woo in muddy pools and gibbons in tall trees.
It really makes me want to itch when I think of mating fleas.

A gander always likes a goose; flies do it on the ceiling.
The rhinoceros's hide is thick so there's very little feeling.

To the woodworm it's so boring in their tiny little holes.
The bat performs by radar and so do garden moles.

Eider drakes are happy when they are feeling down
And Ginger Toms on dustbins like to do it on the Town.

An ibex likes it on the side; of a mountain slope I mean.
The kinkajoo is kinky and the badger's rarely seen.

The salmon travels miles to do it; the caribou's the same.
Hares will do it anywhere and grouse are always game.

Guillemots have fun on rocks; it makes a puffin puff.
If a lady camel takes the hump it means enough's enough.

Lions take a pride in it in Zoos or in the Bush.
Reed warblers in Norfolk find it something of a rush.

Pigeons in Trafalgar Square all do it on the column
But to sparrows in the graveyard it's really rather solemn.

Pandas won't be tempted to do it in the Zoo
But with everybody watching I doubt if you would too.

Well that's the list BUT WATCH IT, for you could have a fright.
That moth up on the lampshade may be taking notes tonight.

Neville Gurnhill,
Skegness.

Mulligan's tyre

Some time ago, Wings had a big hit with 'Mull of Kintyre', a maudlin ditty full of skirling pipes and keening McCartneys. It stayed at No 1 in the Top 20 for what seemed like years, and struck a nerve among many listeners.

There was the bucolic reaction:

Muck in the Byre

There's lots of jobs on the farm I've to do
Some make you happy and some make you blue
Of all of those jobs the one I least desire
Is to clean out the pigs and the muck in the Byre.

Muck in the Byre
Steam rising off the heaps
I desire
To smell something else than the
Muck in the Byre.

John Levison-Wiggins,
Letcombe Regis,
Oxfordshire.

Muck on Kintyre

Muck in the byre
Oh, mist rising up from the greip
My desire
Is always to see heaps
Of muck on Kintyre.

Long have I worked here, much muck have I seen
Spread out on stubble to make fields turn green
Vast middens steaming like they were on fire
As I carry on mucking the byre in Kintyre.

Sweep with my besom clean right the way through
Have the byre spotless and sparkling like new
The cows all a-mooing like some eerie choir
As they deposit their muck on the byre in Kintyre.

Cowpats in sunshine, dung heaps in the rain,
Still at the mucking I think I'll remain,
With the mist from the midden rising higher and higher
As I empty the muck on the Mull of Kintyre.

Anon.

What in heaven's name is a 'greip?' Ray Ellis of Ely, on the other hand, was eager for *me* to climb on the bandwagon:

Dear Terry,
    Herewith please find the words for your next onslaught on the Hit Parade, with congratulations for your last attempts, and condolences for your bad throat – you did have a bad throat when you recorded 'De Plorable Dance,' didn't you?

Molly Kintyre

Molly Kintyre, the miss everyone wants to see.
My desire's not only to *see* her!
Oh! Molly Kintyre.

Far has she travelled – who knows where she's been?
Men come a-running, their eyes all agleam,
Hearts full of passion, consumed with desire
For the lovely, delectable Molly Kintyre.

Ray Ellis,
Ely,
Cambridgeshire.

So was Eileen Mannion of Glasgow:

Mulligan's Tyre (Irish version of McCartney song)

Chorus
Mulligan's tyre
O it's blown a puncture
It's nearly on fire
From friction and much wear
O Mulligan's tyre.

Verse 1
Far has it travelled and much has it seen
Of pebbles and tarmac and grasses so green
Bog land and shamrock and colleens so fair
And it carried them home
It was Mulligan's tyre.

Chorus

Verse 2
Much was it worn yet it carried on
Making the journeys for its leprechaun
Taking the hills through the bog and the mire,
And it would not give in
Not that Mulligan's tyre.

Chorus

Verse 3
Struggling along tho' it was such a strain,
Taking the colleens in sun, wind and rain,
Sadly it blew up going thro' the cow byre,
It had lasted a long time,
That Mulligan's tyre.

Chorus.

**Eileen Mannion,
Glasgow.**

Many pursued the tyre motif, few more successfully than
Steve Knowles of Eastwood, Nottingham:

A Punctured Back Tyre

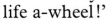ar have I travelled and much have I seen
Broken head gaskets and shattered windscreens
Bashed up front fenders and engines on fire
But all that I get is a punctured back tyre.

Chorus
Punctured back tyre, O why does it happen to me,
My desire is to always be free from a punctured back tyre.

Drive down the M1 and back up again,
Hoping that nothing will happen, but then
A crack from the rear like a pistol shot fire
And it's done it again, I've a punctured back tyre.

Chorus

At last I decided only one thing to do,
I've changed my rotten old four wheels for two
Me and my push-bike go all round the shire,
O my God its just happened, a punctured back tyre.

Chorus.

**Steve Knowles,
Eastwood, Nottingham.**

And yet, as one bi-cyclist enthused to me recently: 'It's a great
life a-wheel!'

The Great Game

Two years ago, I was inveigled to play in the BBC 2 TV series 'Pro-Celebrity Golf'. Came the day, I introduced my morning radio show, caught a plane at 11 o'clock from Heathrow to Glasgow, took a car from Glasgow to glorious Gleneagles, bumped stomachs with Peter Alliss, knocked back a fortifying vodka and tonic, inhaled some of Eric Sykes's cigar smoke and Henry Cooper's perfume and found myself standing on a tee in the heather with Johnny Miller, Tony Jacklin and the jockey Geoff Lewis. I would prefer to draw a veiled sporran over the debacle of missed putts and shanked irons, and the camera zeroing in on me as I took three to get out of the rough.

Suffice it to say that the great Johnny Miller has been in semi-retirement since that fateful day. I marked his card, I am afraid, in more ways than one.

It didn't go unremarked by my listeners either. From the barrage of contumely, this fragrant flower:

Fore

By jove big Tee, you looked the part
All woods, and irons, and big heart
As you strode out with Johnny Miller
In peaked cap you looked a killer.

Indeed you seemed so strong and hale
I composed this poem for your mail
With fifty years' practice, and lots of scouse
You'll be as good as me,

Yours Jack Nick Louse.

> **Pete Floyd,**
> **Carlisle.**

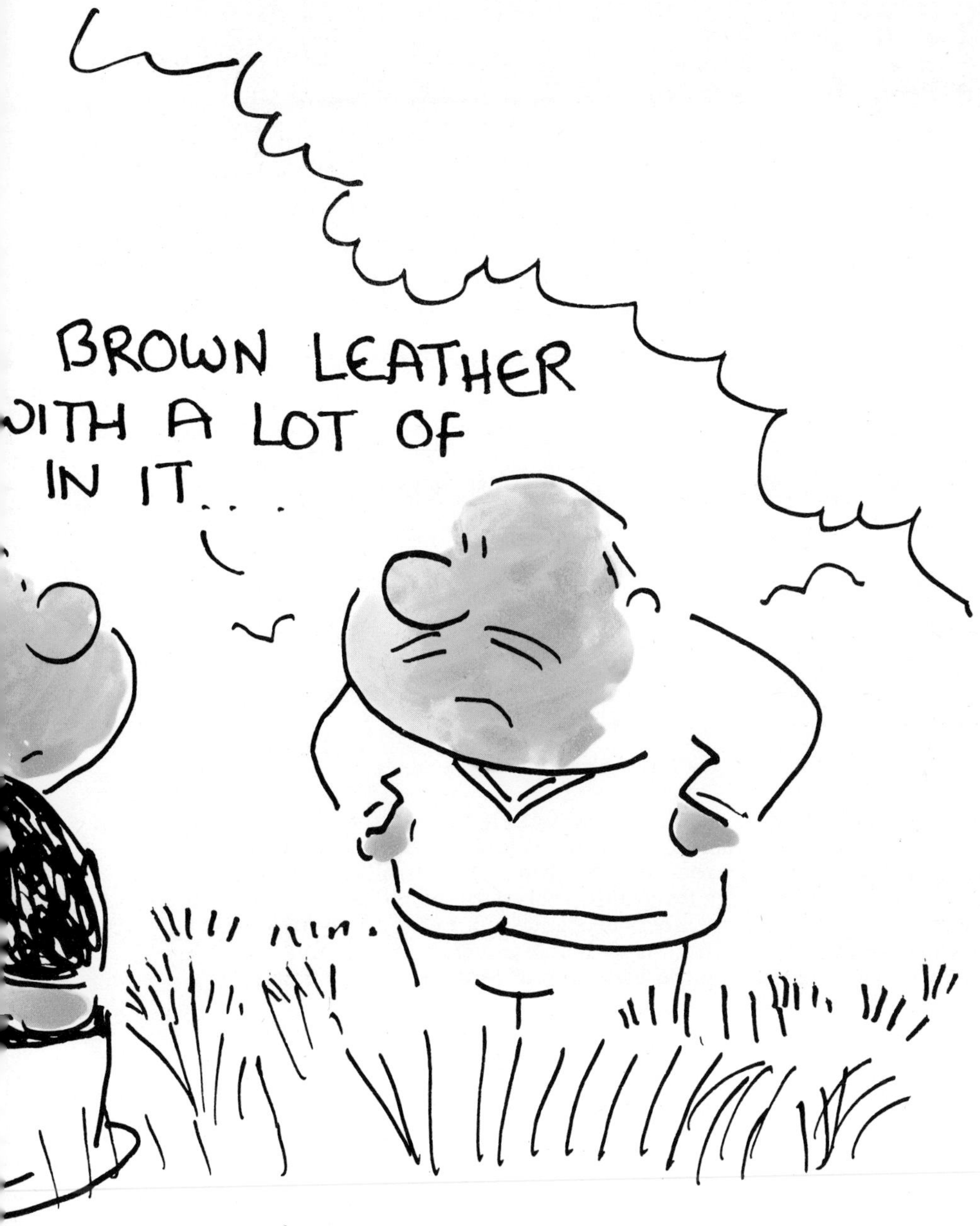
BROWN LEATHER
ITH A LOT OF
IN IT...

Singing in the bath

Perhaps, in a moment of weakness, I may have recalled how my father, Earl Wogan of Ennisberry, used to wake the dead, not to mind the neighbours, intoning 'Many Brave Hearts Lie Asleep in the Deep, so Beware, etc.', as he performed his ablutions. Whatever the excuse, and my listener rarely needs one, it brought this out from behind the bidet:

THE BATHROOM SINGERS ASSOCIATION

Terry Wogan Esq.
BBC,
Broadcasting House,
London W1A 1AA

Head Office
21 Lloyd Square,
London WC1

Dear Mr Wogan,

The Bathroom Singers Association was founded two years ago to link those who like to bellow at the top of their lungs while wallowing in a hot bath and already has a membership of over 100. Membership is open to all devotees of the art and there is a reduced fee for groups such as rugby clubs. In addition to a monthly newsletter members exchange tapes of their performances as well as passing on details of bathrooms with above average resonance – I myself treasure a recording made in the bathroom of Suite 306 at the Savoy Hotel.

As you may imagine, it is not easy for members to have get-togethers but this year we are planning to hire the Albert Hall in September for the first ever Bathroom Singers' wallow. Participants may bring their own baths or may hire one at the Hall for a nominal charge. Dress will be optional, but for those who are somewhat shy a large quantity of bubblebath solution has been kindly donated by a well known manufacturer.

Yours sincerely

David Gordon.

The buck stops here

It is very difficult for the simple broadcaster to open his capacious maw without offending a sensitive listener somewhere. It is hard indeed, having wished the world a bright good morning, to find the BBC switchboard jammed with howls of protest from people on whom the aforementioned morning is sleeting.

As soon as I make idle mention of a nagging ache in the old war wound, waves of protest from veterans of the Ypres Salient lap the very bulwarks of BH (or Broadcasting House, everything in the BBC is referred to by its initials, thus: TVC, Television Centre; HSOB, Head of Sound Outside Broadcasts; there's even someone in darkest Engineering entitled EIEIO! But here! I digress . . .)

Recently, a traffic bulletin brought to my side by the regulation flaxen-haired lovely, carried news of a blockage to Bishopthorpe Road in Hull (or some other jolly spa). This hiatus to traffic continued for some days, and in my winsome yet homely way, I speculated upon the root causes. Whereupon a vicar of the parish explained that it was the drains. At least, initially, it was the drains.

Then it was a search for a camera, which had been put down to photograph what had caused the blockage, and had slipped from the asphyxiated cameraman's fingers into the

MESSAGE FOR WOGAN FROM H.S.O.B

S.W.A.L.K.

morass. I mentioned that unless one was after a chuckle or two, Bishopthorpe Road was a thoroughfare to avoid.

Picture then, if you will, our hero's perplexity on being taken severely to task by a genuinely distressed listener who asked if I was aware that there was a crematorium on Bishopthorpe Road, and that only this very year he had made several trips to it carrying various relations. It seemed to him the height of insensitivity to speak slightingly of Bishopthorpe Road, and he was writing to Equity and the DG.

It's not only my own gaffes for which I take the rap, either. On a recent TV ballroom-dancing spectacular, which I introduced, some young lady flourished a Union Jack upside down, and I received an incensed letter from a Brownie to say that neither she nor the rest of her pack would ever watch or listen to me again!

I'm also expected to be a watchdog:

Dear Mr Wogan,
As the presenter of 'Blankety Blank', the programme synonymous with Truth and Justice, can you please confirm our worst suspicions. Is it true that Hugh Scully was sucking a sweet, halfway through 'Nationwide' on Wednesday last, 2nd May.

Mrs Maureen Grage,
Ware, Hertfordshire.

Luckily, Scully can stand up for himself:

Dear Terry, Sir, I must admit
That Scully has been rumbled
And I'll make a clean breast of it,
To your listener who grumbled.

But in self defence I must point out
It wasn't quite as she described –
Not a sweetie in my mouth that night,
But a medicinal pastille, as prescribed.

The BBC has doctors, and lovely nurses too,
And when my voice was cracking up,
They said here's a lozenge you can chew.

Hugh Scully,
'Nationwide'.

A likely story.

Further contumely

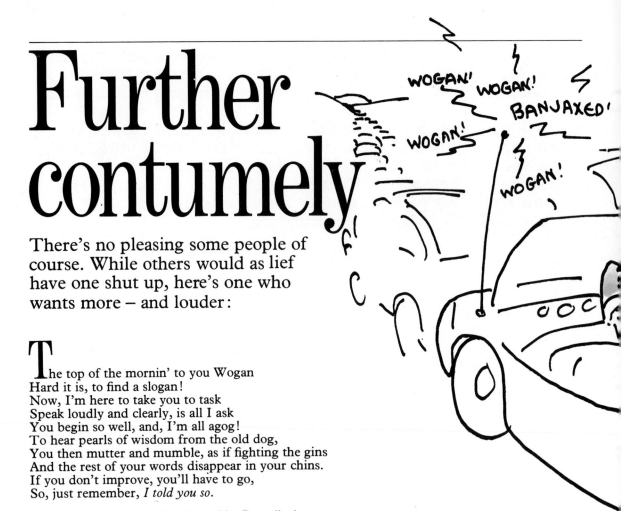

There's no pleasing some people of course. While others would as lief have one shut up, here's one who wants more – and louder:

The top of the mornin' to you Wogan
Hard it is, to find a slogan!
Now, I'm here to take you to task
Speak loudly and clearly, is all I ask
You begin so well, and, I'm all agog!
To hear pearls of wisdom from the old dog,
You then mutter and mumble, as if fighting the gins
And the rest of your words disappear in your chins.
If you don't improve, you'll have to go,
So, just remember, *I told you so.*

'The Devonshire Dumpling'.

While others, more fortunate, receive cheery postcards from foreign parts wishing they were there, I get this, from Tenerife:

Dear Terry Wogan,
I'm sat here looking out over a sun kissed sea basking in the peace and tranquillity of not being able to receive your programme (it's like relief from toothache). Put my Manchester YMCA tee-shirt on every day, thought I might see you here fighting your tremendous fat. Still, back to the grind of your programme next week.

Ian.

It all makes a person feel wanted. However, I have to admit that I *do* get the odd friendly card; mostly, it appears, from listeners passing through Dallas, Texas (for reasons discussed earlier). These show heartening views of the town's soaring skyline, and speak highly of its vital culture and throbbing commerciality. Fair enough, but I could do without each card's centre piece – a detailed plan of how and where the late J F Kennedy was shot. A pretty macabre tourist attraction!

I've always believed that there's much more fun to be derived from critical letters than laudatory ones – particularly when you get this kind of thing:

D ear Sir,
THE TERRY WOGAN SHOW
I am sorry to say that something has gone
wrong with the radio in my car so that I can
only receive Radio 2 without undue
interference. Even on this programme, it is sad
that I get worse interference in the name of
Terry Wogan.

Often when driving to work I like to
listen to something a little more light hearted
than Radio 4 complete with sensible people.
However, like most others I am unfortunate
enough to have to tune in to Terry Wogan.
It is obvious that Mr Wogan is just about the
corniest and lowest quality broadcaster ever to
step inside the BBC. It is a pity you have a
monopoly otherwise you would not last long,
as with TV.

I don't suppose Mr Wogan will see this
letter; in any event he would be too conceited
to look at it for too long or certainly take any
notice of it. It is not only me, but many of my
friends who simply cannot stand Mr Wogan
first thing on a Monday morning.

It's noticeable that, in all critical letters, people never speak for just themselves, but also for their many discerning friends. What made it all worthwhile, though, was the handwritten note attached to the above:

Dear Sir,
           'The Terry Wogan Show'
It was unfortunately part of my secretarial
duties today to type a somewhat rude, not to
say occasionally ungrammatical letter
concerning Mr Wogan from my employer. The
latter is usually an even tempered and even
considerate man but I must put pen to paper
to state that I firmly disagree with the contents
of his letter and positively *enjoy* listening to
Mr Wogan!

**Mrs E Vaughan,
Canon Pyon, Hereford.**

So there.

The all-round entertainer

In my never-ending crusade to push the frontiers of radio forward, to boldly go where broadcaster has never been, etc., etc., I have experimented with various forms of 'visual' entertainment, which previously had been thought unworkable on radio. Who was the first to do the Indian rope-trick on the wireless? And tap-dancing? Who interviewed a magician, who made a pound note disappear before the listeners' very eyes? Who staged the Battle of the River Plate one afternoon on Radios 1 and 2? And who cares?

Rarely, however, has a facet of my versatility taken my listeners' breath away to such an extent as my recent 'juggling' display. This was done with three special juggling balls, sent me by some benign juggler, and I think what impressed even the most hardened listener was that I kept them in the air, while balancing on one hand, without ever losing the even tenor of my broadcast.

Herewith, modestly and fine-featured, a selection of the stunned reaction:

HE'S KEEPING THEM IN THE AIR BUT HE'S NOT THROWING THEM VERY HIGH...

Dear Mr Wogan – Sir!

Is there no limit to your talent? Does the DG realize your full potential?

I was impressed by your incredible juggling feat and am convinced that with the right training you could become the world's first gymnastics champion of the air. Let's face it – you have the figure for it!

My son (who is otherwise an intelligent child) doesn't believe you really juggled with three balls whilst balancing on one hand – the young have no faith – and wants you to repeat it on 'Blankety Blank'.

Margaret George,
Earith, Cambridgeshire.

PS. Have you noticed how all the best people are called 'Margaret' lately?

Dear Terry,

I was thrilled to hear your juggling first thing in the morning. The dexterous way you handled those balls was sweet music to my ears.

To help you excel your past performances I feel sure a blindfold juggling session would be-dazzle all your thousand and one listeners, so please use the enclosed blindfold and astonish us once again.

Have you ever thought that with Jimmy Young's help you could have a three-legged juggling race.

Mrs Margaret Tote,
Skegness, Lincolnshire.

Dear Mr Wogan,

I enjoyed your Wednesday morning cabaret very much – not often you get a good juggling act on the radio these days. Why don't you do a few conjuring tricks as well and get the DG to assist you? You could get him to pick a card – then show it to the listeners!

Better still – do a few illusions, such as disappearing off the radio completely!!!!

Bryan Rhodes-Smith,
Addlestone, Surrey.

Mrs Tote very kindly enclosed a transparent plastic bag for a blindfold. Such thoughtfulness. Of course, you'll always have the begrudger:

I was very pleased to hear your juggling,' wrote one gentleman, 'because you were quiet for a few moments, and it shut out your outrageously boring cackle . . .'

Do you think Sammy Davis Jr has to put up with this?

The Albanians are coming

Heaven knows, it's not for me, a lowly disc-jockey, to speculate on the Machiavellian machinations that led to The Great Wavelength Switch of 23 November 1978. Many blamed the EEC, others The Gang of Four, still more President Carter's brother Billy, but ● A Man Who Should Know told me that it was all the fault of the Albanians, jumping up and down on everybody else's wavelengths.as if the air were free.

Suffice it to say that few events in broadcasting have led to such schism and doubt among the unfortunate listeners. People accustomed to being ● cossetted by my dulcet tones of an early morning were suddenly assaulted by Redhead, Timpson and Purves, a little-known firm of undertakers. Radio 4 came through clear as a bell in Cracow, and muffled in Middlesex; Nancy Wise turned into Jimmy Young; Tony Blackburn began to worry the sheep in the Outer Hebrides; and they've put out a dragnet for Radio 3.

On the eve of the Great Disappearing Trick, Roger Mitchell, the Bard of Jersey, penned these prophetic tones:

Ode on the Eve of St Jude th'Obscure (23 November)

Now is the winter of our discontent
Made cold Siberia by the Great DG
And those of us who dallied with the Wog
And sported with him in the summer days
Have had him dashed from us for evermore.
No more shall Wogan's Winner prance the turf
Nor loads abnormal pass the motorways.
And gentlemen in Europe now abed
Shall think themselves accursed they cannot hear
And hold their manhood cheap while any speaks
That knew of Terry Wogan in his prime.
Tomorrow is the feast of Jude th'Obscure
The patron Saint of causes failed and lost.
He that shall live this day and see old age
Will yearly on the vigil drink his wine
And say 'Tomorrow is St Jude th'Obscure'
For though the British Isles will hear our lad
He will be barred from those inContinent.

**Roger Mitchell,
Jersey.**

LISTEN TO THOSE DAMNED ALBANIANS !!

Others, like Vic Jarvis, saw it as the culmination of plotting in High Places to see *me* finally off the premises:

Farewell

The time is fast approaching,
For the parting of the waves,
I hear you're finally going,
After several narrow shaves.

The DG's been round with his ruler,
So for you, Sir, this is it,
Whilst you're alright for the long wave,
In the medium you'll never fit.

No more shall we hear the chatter,
That makes all your listeners fidget,
On the twenty-third of November,
You're being replaced by a midget!

We wish you well on your going,
A sad dejected soul,
I hear the money's not too bad,
For those upon the dole.

Your Fan Club will be disbanded,
That gallant band of three,
So it's farewell from we stalwarts,
Your Mother, the Duck, and me!

**Vic Jarvis,
Forest Hill.**

Gone, gone – and never called me 'Mother'.

Metrication

So wrapped up were we, selfish broadcasters, in confusing the listeners by leaping from medium to long wave, and back again, that it took a letter from Dr Geoffrey Horton to bring us down to earth and point to Even Bigger Issues:

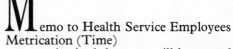

M

emo to Health Service Employees
Metrication (Time)

As doubtless you will have read in the national press, from midnight on 3 January 1979 the whole of Great Britain (except the Isle of Man) will be converted to metric time.

From that date there will be 10 seconds to the minute, 10 minutes to the hour, 10 hours to the day and so on, delineated according to the following table.

Old Time New Time

Old Time	New Time
1 second	= 1 milliday
1 minute	= 1 centiday
1 hour	= 1 deciday (or millimonth)
1 day	= 1 day
1 week	= 1 decaday
1 month	= 1 hectaday
1 year	= 1 kiloday

The fortnight will be withdrawn.

Due to the fact that 1 new hour represents only 5/12 of an old hour, employees will be expected to work longer hours, viz $3\frac{1}{2}$ decidays or millimonths per day.

It is not expected at this time that any compensatory uplift will be made to wages except in the case of leap kilodays when an adjustment will be built in at the end of the hectaday every 1.46 decamonths.

The pension schemes will not be affected but superkilodayvaluation will be adjusted accordingly.

Holidays will be affected only so far as the change to metric time is concerned and no one shall be worse off than before. Thus if an employee was entitled to 22 days (Old Time) he will now be entitled to 220 decidays or one hectaday plus 20 decidays for every hectaday over and above 20 kilodays' service since the 10th deciday of the third hectaday of 1979.

Special holidays will be accordingly reduced to 5 decidays but 10 demi-decadays will be added where relevant to the Christmas break which will be moved to the August Bank Holiday to take advantage of the longer shopping decidays.

Metric Time Conversion Tables are available from the British Standards Institute, the Department of Health and Social Security and at all British Rail Booking Offices.

Dr Geoffrey Horton,
Edwinstowe, Nottinghamshire.

And you think it can't happen?

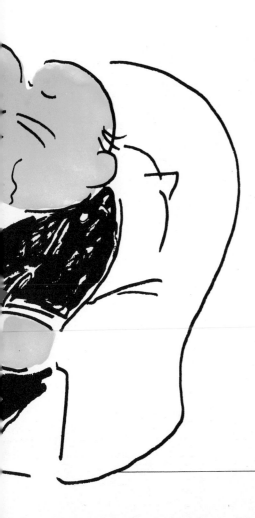

Belabour the blubber

He who labours under the delusion that jogging is mainly an American disease ought to take an early-morning stroll along Portland Place, London. He'll want to keep his wits about him, though, to avoid being trampled underfoot by the entire staff of the Embassy of the Chinese People's Republic, as they hurtle up to Regents Park to terrify the ducks.

From 6 to 8 every morning, the very pavements tremble to the heavy trot of rising executives, wobbly matrons, and middle management bashing the blood-pressure, also silver-haired members of the medical profession who ought to know better. The gutters are choked with sweat-stained bodies in track-suits fighting for breath, the air is full of rasping coughs, wheezes and, all too often, death-rattles.

Suddenly, from the tradesmen's entrance of the BBC a pathetic figure launches himself into this landscape of blood, sweat and tears. In open-toed sandals, grey anklesocks, khaki shorts that

QUACK!   QUACK!   QUACK!

droop below the knee and a disgraceful vest bearing the legend 'Property of Wormwood Scrubs, Do Not Remove', the shambling figure makes his way down Regent Street. Who can it be? you cry. Oh, come on! Do you really *need* to ask?

The Low-down on the BBC Roof

I'll tell you a tale of the 'Beeb' lads
Where they play all the latest hits
And that harsh rending sound
You can hear from the ground
Is the DG performing the splits.

Yes, he's up on the roof keeping fit lads
While most are just taking a rest
He's cavorting about
Disregarding his gout
In a filthy old ankle-length vest.

Ah! But what is that terrible smell lads?
From that shed almost hidden from view.
Hang your heads in disgrace
For this is the place
Where they melt Wogan's Winners for glue!

Anon.

Wogan's Winner

'That slighting reference on the previous page to 'Wogan's Winner' is, of course, just another in a long line of despicable slurs. This time on my abilities as a tipster, a Man of The Turf, a Son of The Ould Sod.

It sometimes seems to me that I can scarce stick my head out through the portcullis of a morning without some ribald wit shouting, 'Tip winners? You couldn't tip rubbish!' Or some other polished shaft, such as, 'Ere! 'ow much are the bookies payin' you, then?' Naturally, I treat these crude jibes with the haughty scorn they deserve, but beneath the patrician mask the words wound. Of course, I would like to think that Joe Coral will not want for anything, and that Mrs William Hill is being kept in the comfort to which she has become accustomed, but, friends, I am out to banjax the bookies, terrorize the turf accountants, and bring home the bacon for the punter in the street.

I've obviously got them on the run if this sign, sent me by a loyal listener from his local bookie's office, is anything to go by:

Whistling into the wind, I call it.

The Racing Information Bulletin was being broadcast every morning on Radio 2 at 8.27 am long before I was even a glimmer in the granny's eye. When I took over, to the groans of the discerning listener, some bright spark had the idea that I should end each bulletin with a tip for the day, to be called 'Wogan's Winner'. And so, through dungeon, fire and sword, it has remained. I've never pretended to know the first thing about horses, or racing, so the tip is provided every day by my good friends from the Racing Information Bureau. And notwithstanding the stick I take from taxi-drivers, waitresses and refuse disposal operatives, our record over seven years has been no worse, and in some cases a great deal better, than that of any other tipster. Indeed, I have been known to top the money-winning tipster's table! Not for long, mind you.

However, the idea persists that Wogan's Winner is a Loser, and that to be selected for the honour is as the Kiss of Death. And that's the way I like it. I have no wish to be accused of undermining the moral fibre of the nation by encouraging the listener to hurl the last of the children's allowance on the back of some spavined nag.

Indeed, I stand exonerated, while other tipsters get the knife in the small ribs, by no less a body than the World Council of Churches, with their 'Report on Gambling'. My activities as a horse-race tipster, it was felt, should be encouraged by all right-thinking people, as my tips constituted a positive discouragement to gambling.

It's rather like all these 'complimentary' letters I get, that start: 'Dear Terry, I always stand up for you, when the rest of the factory starts criticizing . . .'

Wagan's Woger

Handsome animal isn't he? Proud head, strong thews, good temperament, glossy coat, and trained to an hair. The horse looks pretty good, too, considering it's had to live with the unequal burden of a monniker like Wogan's Wager. Mark the look of barely concealed disdain on the creature's face as it correctly diagnoses that the human (the one in the ill-fitting suit) is poised for flight, if it so much as twitches an ear.

Call me a sissy if you like, but I've always been apprehensive of anything that's got more legs than me, iron hooves, and teeth like a mowing machine. Horses recognize this immediately of course, and on sight of me usually give a couple of cheeky neighs, a swish of the tail, and chase me round the paddock until my six-year-old daughter comes to rescue me.

I must have been somewhat tired and emotional therefore, when I agreed to take a share in this horse. It wasn't much – an half a fetlock I think, but they named the poor dumb animal after me. Enough, you would have said, to stunt anything's growth. And you would have been correct in every detail. This snap was taken when the horse was two years old, and despite eating its head off with oats, nuts and the finest of equine delicacies it never grew so much as a finger, not to mind an hand, after this picture was taken. It's this strange power I have over animals and women . . .

Wogan's Wager had a couple of runs, without breaking into a canter, or indeed a sweat, before I went to see him race for the first time 'neath the ancient city walls of Chester, on the famed Roodeye course. An air of quiet confidence prevailed in the Wogan camp and was maintained right up to the moment when little WW strolled out of the starting gate, and took up a comfortable position 100 yards behind the rest of the field, loping easily. It was a position he held without much trouble for the entire race and the game little chap finished unflurried, and last, with the satisfied air of one who realizes that it's not the winning that counts, but the taking part.

That was bad enough, but the crowning blow to my budding career as another Aga Khan or Wildenstein came as the horses rounded the final bend. 'And last at the moment,' roared the race commentator to the packed stands, 'last is Wagan's Woger.' I fancy I can hear the ribald jeering yet.

The little horse continued to enjoy the view of other horses disappearing out of sight in front of him, and eventually, because the cardboard soles of my children's shoes would scarce have lasted another winter, I sold my interest in Wogan's Wager. He immediately won three races in succession, at 25–1, 100–8, and 3–1. Lucky Wogan, they call me.

Wise quacks

Once, there was a record by The Goodies, entitled 'A Man's Best Friend Is His Duck', which contained such deathless lines as 'It can give you a nasty suck'. Rejoicing that the spirit of Ivor Novello yet lived on, I played it often. I might have known what it would lead to:

Quacking Jokes

What is a piece of repartee? — A wisequack

What do political ducks do? — Paper over the quacks

What is a glamorous duckling? — A quacker, a bit of quackling

What is a crazy duck? — A quackpot

Which would you choose between two ducks? — Eider

How does one exhort a duck to action? — 'Get quacking!'

**Audrey Hundy,
Worcestershire.**

Naturally, this aroused the clergy:

Duck Jokes

What do you get when you cross a worm with a duck? — An earthquack

What does a duck eat for breakfast? — Quacker Oats

Which is a duck's favourite television programme? — Quackerjack

What is suitable music for a mentally deficient charming little duck? — Nut Quacker Sweet.

**Revd Edward Barrow,
Guildford, Surrey.**

And a gagster from Norfolk called Neep:

What do you call a cat that's eaten a duck? — A duck-filled-fatty-puss.

**Mervyn Neep,
St Germans, Norfolk.**

My old friend Harold Jones, of Clwyd, was not to be left out:

Ducks

What is a male French duck? Mongoose
Poise is behaving like a duck: keeping calm and unruffled on the surface
but paddling like the devil underneath.
When the baby duckling had a lift across the farmyard, it was viaduct.

Harold Jones,
Rhyl, Clwyd.

As always, in this fur-and-feather-loving land, there was someone to remind us of the debt that we owe to ducks:

Dear Mr Wogan,
Please refrain from taking the mickey out of ducks. I would remind you
that they performed valuable wartime service in Q-ack Q-ack batteries and
shot down many enemy carrier pigeons.

Yours buoyantly
Donald Ducati
The Pond,
Bury, Lancashire.

And people wonder why I need a holiday.

Make mine 'Country' style

'Country and Western' became just 'Country' music some years back when I wasn't looking, but, pards, I jest caint control the rebel yell that comes a-bubblin' to my lips whenever I hear that good ol' fiddle and banjo. 'Eeee-Hah!' I go, and it drives the more ethnically minded country music fan bananas. It appears that my coarse yelling is not treating a very serious art-form with the dignity it deserves. However, last year I was the winner of the Country Music Association's award for 'Non-Country Specialist', and I'm proud of it, whatever it may mean.

Country music is alive with ringing names: Moe Bandy, Conway Twitty, Boxcar Willie, Porter Waggoner. Among the gals, there's Billie Jo Spears (The Singing Harpoon) and that musical depression centred over Iceland, Crystal Gayle; Dolly Parton defies the law of gravity every time she takes a deep breath, and Tammy Wynette will not easily be forgotten, if only for that deathless spelling bee, 'D.I.V.O.R.C.E.' What other popular music form would even attempt such titles as 'St Louis Named a Shoe After Me' or 'Jeremiah Peabody's Polyunsaturated Quick Dissolving, Fast Acting, Pleasant Tasting, Green and Purple Pills'?

'Lucille' was a big country hit for Kenny Rogers – a touching tale of a woman leaving her man in the lurch: 'You picked a fine time to leave me, Lucille, With four hungry children and a crop in the field . . .' These sentiments may well have struck a responsive chord among the softies who listen to other radio shows, but not my crowd. Their reaction, to a man, was roundly to applaud the woman: 'It's no wonder she left him – four hundred children and a croc in the field. Typical selfish male chauvinist!'

The nude vicar

'Lucille' is only one of a myriad songs that the ever-vigilant British listening public has deliberately and delightedly macerated. That soulful ballad 'Love Grows Where My Rosemary Goes' quickly became 'Love Grows Up My Rosemary's Nose' – a very sore thing.

Neil Diamond recently had a success with 'Forever In Blue Jeans', which attracted an hearty response from the minor clergy, who seemed to take it as a tribute to swinging vicars everywhere – 'The Reverend Blue Jeans'. This same worthy band took exception to my condolences to someone in hospital. In my manly yet cuddly way, I wished some patient well, and expressed the hope that he or she would shortly be sitting up, and taking the lightly boiled egg with 'renewed vigour'. How they could possibly misconstrue this as encouraging someone to tuck into breakfast with a 'nude vicar' is beyond me.

FOR WHAT WE ARE ABOUT TO RECEIVE

D ear Mr Wogan,
Your remarks regarding patients in hospital attacking the lightly boiled egg with a nude vicar. This is a slur on us vicars who are hard-boiled and fully clothed.

**Ivor Pulpit,
St Albans.**

It's partly the singers' fault, of course. Karen Carpenter's nasal tones *did* make it seem as if 'The best love songs are written with a broken arm'. 'Broken *heart*' was what the songwriter had in mind. Then there was Stu Stevens – 'The Man from Outer Space': disillusioned with Earth and bungling *homo sapiens,* he sang 'I'm leaving in the morning on a blue electric loo . . .' At least that's what it sounded like to my gang.

Ishar Cohen and Alphabeta won the Eurovision Song Contest for Israel in 1978, with a catchy farrago called 'Ah Ba Ni Bi'; apparently, my name is mud with the bold Ishar because I 'sent it up'. Me? I ask you. Anyway, I blame the listeners, your honour. The first line of this epic went something like: 'Ah Ba Ni Bi, Ah Bo Na Beh'. Hardly Noel Coward, I admit, but well up to Eurovision Song Contest standards. Nothing could dislodge from my listeners' minds the quaint idea that what Ishar and the boys were singing was 'I wanna be a polar bear'. This in turn led to some tiring, but erudite, exposition:

To the handsomest, wittiest, most talented
DJ on Radio.
Terry Wogan for King and Jimmy Young
for Queen!
Dear Sir Terry,
        Just practising, you are right, it is polar
bear. In fact the lyric is as British as tatty bogles.
Tis a true story passed down from hand to
mouth over the generations. My great great
uncle seventeen times removed – poet,
poacher and beekeeper extraordinaire
produced a non-sticky honey, which Good
Queen Bess massaged into her scalp to
titillate the follicles. The result gave her
much pleasure until alas one day the
promiscuous queen bee went bananas over a
brazen bumble in the next hive, and
jammed up the juice. Resulting in a bald
bonce for 'Liz' R, and a quick trip to the
Tower for my bemused ancestor.
        Anticipating the chop, he dashed off
a quick sonnet which her Majesty duly
censored, issuing a Royal Warrant that
anyone uttering a word of the said verse
would follow the author.
        However, his wife, wishing to make
a quick ducat out of his misfortune, flogged
a few illicit copies and one found itself you
know where! The real version goes thus:
Ye Barmy Barmy Bee,
What hast thou done to me,
Thy misdemeanor hast my Queen undone,
Her flaming hair she's lost,
So in the Tower I'm tossed,
I wonder where the polar bears have gone.
        The last line was coded; alas we will
never know what it meant.

Grace Whitby,
Derby.

Ban'jax vt Middle Irish (cf Dineen).
To hornswoggle, corpse, knacker, rasher,
caramelize, malafooster, malavogue,
powfagg, keelhaul, macerate, decimate,
pulverize, make rawmeish of. Hence
Banjaxed, reduced to the condition of a
pig's breakfast, and **Banjaxing,** tearing a
plaster from an hairy leg.